The Art of War

The Posters of World War II

Sean Price

Chicago, Illinois

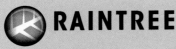
RAINTREE

TO ORDER:
☎ Phone Customer Service **888-454-2279**
💻 Visit **www.heinemannraintree.com** to browse our catalog and order online.

©2009 Raintree
a division of Pearson Education Limited
Chicago, Illinois

Editorial: Adam Miller
Design: Ryan Frieson, Kimberly R. Miracle,
  and Betsy Wernert
Photo Research: Tracy Cummins
Production: Victoria Fitzgerald

Originated by DOT Gradations Ltd
Printed and bound by Leo Paper Group

ISBN-13: 978-1-4109-3114-6 (hc)
ISBN-10: 1-4109-3114-5 (hc)
ISBN-13: 978-1-4109-3123-8 (pb)
ISBN-10: 1-4109-3123-4 (pb)

13 12 11 10 09
10 9 8 7 6 5 4 3 2 1

Library of Congress Cataloging-in-Publication Data
Price, Sean.
  The art of war : the posters of World War II / Sean Price.
    p. cm. -- (American history through primary sources)
  Includes bibliographical references and index.
  ISBN 978-1-4109-3114-6 (hc) -- ISBN 978-1-4109-
3123-8 (pb) 1. World War, 1939-1945--Posters--Juvenile
literature. 2. World War, 1939-1945--United States--
Juvenile literature. I. Title. II. Title: Posters of World War II.
III. Title: Posters of World War Two. IV. Title: Posters of World
War 2.
  D743.25.P75 2008
  940.54'886730222--dc22
                    2008011295

Acknowledgments
The author and publisher are grateful to the following
for permission to reproduced copyright material: ©The
Art Archive **pp. 24** (Imperial War Museum), **25**; ©Corbis
pp. **4** (Bettmann), **7** (David Pollack), **14** (Bettmann), **23**;
©Gettty Images/Fox Photos **p. 6**; ©Library of Congress
Prints and Photographs Division **pp. 5, 9-B, 9-T, 10, 11,
12, 13-B, 13-T, 15, 17, 18, 19, 22, 28, 29**; ©National
Archives **pp. 8, 16, 26, 27**; ©Printed by permission of
the Norman Rockwell Family Agency Copyright © 1943
Norman Rockwell Family Entities **p. 21**.

Cover image of the "Stay On the Job" poster (1941–
1945), used with permission of ©National Archives and
©Shutterstock (for the background).

The publishers would like to thank Nancy Harris for her
assistance in the preparation of this book.

Every effort has been made to contact copyright holders
of any material reproduced in this book. Any omissions
will be rectified in subsequent printings if notice is given
to the publisher.

Contents

Some words are printed in bold, **like this**. You can find out what they mean on page 30.

A World at War

September 1, 1939, was a terrible day. People in the country of Poland woke to the sound of gunfire. They heard cannons boom. Airplanes appeared in the sky. The planes dropped bombs.

World War II had begun. People in Poland saw the first battles. But the war would soon spread worldwide. The fighting would last until 1945.

Germany started the war. Germany was a country next door to Poland (see map on page 6). Germany was run by Adolf Hitler. He believed Germans should take over Poland. He wanted Germans to control the world. But other countries stood up to Germany.

German planes like this one bombed Poland. This happened in May of 1940.

This poster asks young Germans to attend Hitler's youth camp.

Posters were a common sight during the war. Posters were used to share ideas. Posters also explained why people should fight. They helped keep people strong through hard times.

The poster on this page is from Germany. It tells young people to follow Hitler. This book has many other posters as well. They will show you what life was like during World War II.

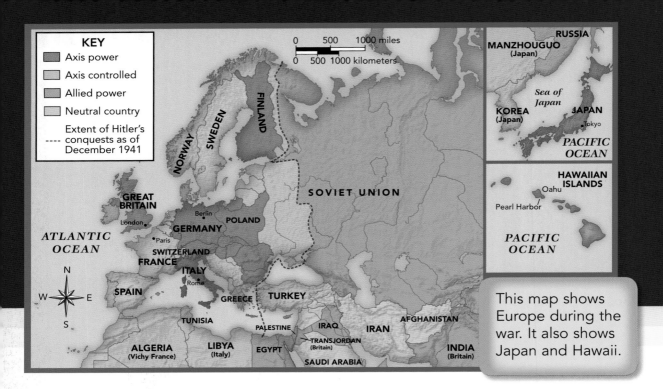

0   500   1000 miles
0   500 1000 kilometers

RUSSIA

MANZHOUGUO (Japan)

Sea of Japan

KOREA (Japan)

JAPAN

Tokyo

PACIFIC OCEAN

HAWAIIAN ISLANDS

Oahu

Pearl Harbor

PACIFIC OCEAN

NORWAY

SWEDEN

FINLAND

SOVIET UNION

GREAT BRITAIN

London

Berlin

POLAND

GERMANY

Paris

SWITZERLAND

FRANCE

ITALY

Rome

ATLANTIC OCEAN

N
W   E
S

SPAIN

GREECE

TURKEY

TUNISIA

PALESTINE

IRAQ

TRANSJORDAN (Britain)

IRAN

AFGHANISTAN

ALGERIA (Vichy France)

LIBYA (Italy)

EGYPT

SAUDI ARABIA

INDIA (Britain)

This map shows Europe during the war. It also shows Japan and Hawaii.

Britain stands alone

Hitler's armies did well at first. They took over Poland. They took over other countries as well. Some countries tried to stop Hitler. But things looked bad for them early in the war. By July 1940, only Great Britain stood against Germany.

Great Britain is on a group of islands. Hitler could not attack the islands easily. Instead, he sent planes to attack Great Britain. The British were led by Winston Churchill. He urged his people to fight on. They did. The British had few planes. But they shot down many German planes. Hitler had to stop sending planes over Great Britain. He could not invade Great Britain. His soldiers would be killed by the British planes.

This picture shows London after a bombing. German planes bombed many cities in Great Britain.

Winston Churchill lead Britain during the war. He tried to make people join together to stand up to Germany.

"LET US GO FORWARD TOGETHER"

Hitler did have friends. The countries of Japan and Italy took his side. With Germany, they formed the **Axis** Powers. Other countries sided with Great Britain. They were called the **Allies**. In 1941, the **Soviet Union** (now Russia) joined the Allies. So did the United States of America.

Axis	countries that sided with Hitler during World War II. Germany, Italy, and Japan led the Axis powers.
Allies	countries that sided with Great Britain during World War II. Great Britain, the Soviet Union, and the United States led Allied forces.
Soviet Union	very large country that broke into many countries in 1991. The

Pearl Harbor

Most Americans wanted to stay out of World War II. The war was being fought far away. Americans saw it as someone else's fight.

But that changed on December 7, 1941. Japanese airplanes attacked Pearl Harbor. Pearl Harbor is in Hawaii. The Japanese sank many U.S. warships there.

Americans were shocked. They were angry. They wanted to get back at Japan. Soon, Germany also declared war on the United States. That made Americans angry, too.

The U.S. government wanted people to stay angry at Japan and the **Axis** Powers (see map on page 6). It wanted to remind people why they were fighting. So many U.S. posters said "Remember Pearl Harbor."

Japanese planes destroyed U.S. warships at Pearl Harbor. Many soldiers lost their lives.

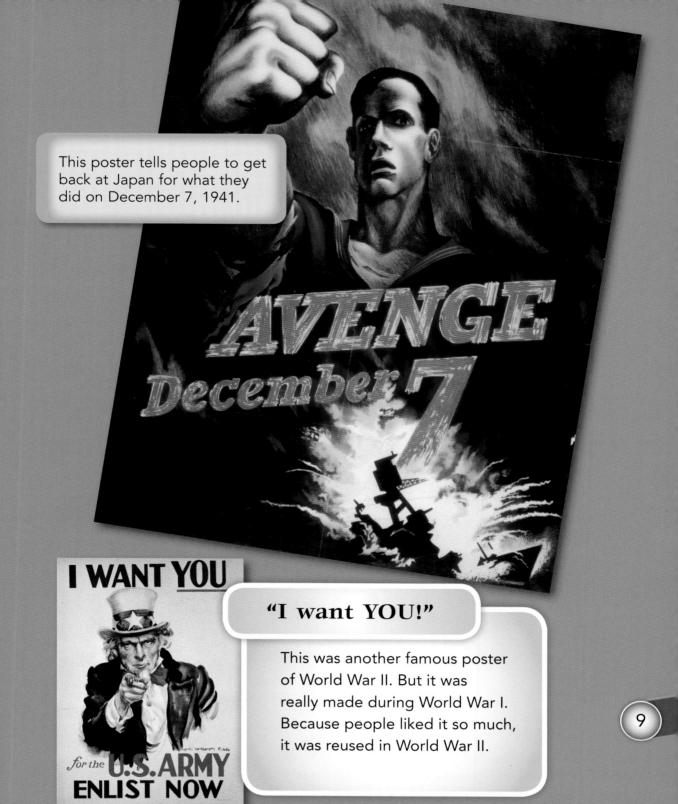

This poster tells people to get back at Japan for what they did on December 7, 1941.

AVENGE December 7

I WANT YOU

"I want YOU!"

This was another famous poster of World War II. But it was really made during World War I. Because people liked it so much, it was reused in World War II.

for the U.S. ARMY ENLIST NOW

The Home Front

World War II was fought in many places. Wherever fighting took place was called the "front lines."

Most Americans lived far from the fighting. People called life at home "the **home front**." A lot of Americans on the home front worked in factories. Those factories made bullets and bombs. They made airplanes and ships. These weapons were used to fight on the front lines.

Back then, most women worked at home. They raised children. They cooked and cleaned house. Jobs outside the home were given to men.

Posters like this asked women to leave home and do wartime work.

The more WOMEN at work the sooner we WIN!

WOMEN ARE NEEDED ALSO AS:

FARM WORKERS	WAITRESSES	TIMEKEEPERS	LAUNDRESSES
TYPISTS	BUS DRIVERS	ELEVATOR OPERATORS	TEACHERS
SALESPEOPLE	TAXI DRIVERS	MESSENGERS	CONDUCTORS

— and in hundreds of other war jobs!

SEE YOUR LOCAL U.S. EMPLOYMENT SERVICE

This woman is working on a U.S. bomber plane.

But that changed during the war. Men were expected to fight. Most young men left. They went into the army or navy. That left too few men to work on the home front.

So women began doing the work. They got jobs in factories. They built airplanes and ships. They made bullets and bombs. Posters urged women to work in factories. Women also drove buses and trains. They did jobs that were once set aside for men.

Doing without

U.S. soldiers needed metal for bullets. They needed leather for boots. On the **home front** (at home), metal and leather were rationed. That meant Americans could only buy these items in small amounts.

Many items were **rationed** (see list on page 13). Sugar was one of them. Most U.S. sugar came from overseas. Ships had to bring it into the U.S. But those ships were now needed for the war. So Americans had less sugar to buy.

FOOD will WIN the WAR

Food was needed for the war, too.

What was rationed?

Here are a few rationed items:

Tires	Sugar
Cars	Coffee
Bicycles	Meat
Gasoline	Fish
Rubber products	Cheese
Shoes	

Americans had to use ration books like this to buy many things.

Other types of food were rationed as well. Posters asked people to grow "**Victory Gardens**." These gardens let them grow their own food.

Americans used old items until they wore out. There was a popular saying: "Use it up, wear it out, make it do, or do without."

Posters like this made Americans on the home front want to grow their own food. That way, there would be more food to send to the soldiers.

Write to me often

Soldiers loved to get mail. Most soldiers were far from home. Many were away for the first time. A letter reminded them of loved ones. It lifted their spirits. One American said, "A soldier's life revolves around his mail."

Soldiers mailed lots of letters. So did their families. But sending all these letters was expensive. One letter is light. But many letters together can be very heavy. Planes and ships had to carry the letters. The army and navy looked for ways to make the letters lighter. That would take fewer planes and ships.

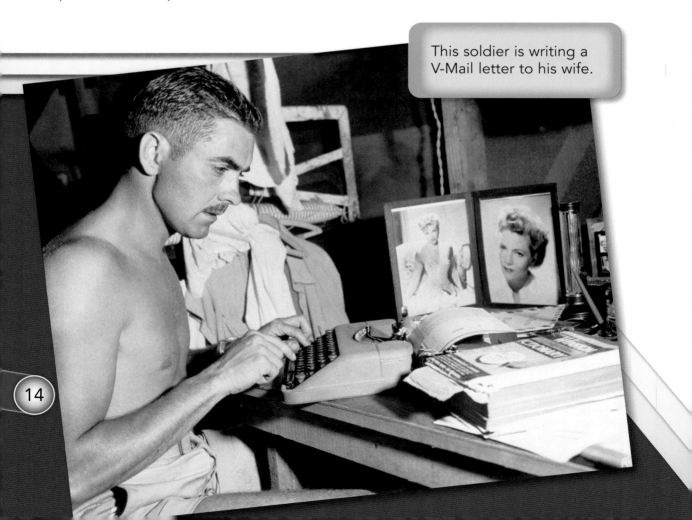

This soldier is writing a V-Mail letter to his wife.

Posters asked people to use **V-Mail**. The V stood for "Victory." V-Mail was sent in a special way. After it was mailed, each letter was photographed. Then the photograph was shrunk. It was shrunk to the size of a thumb nail. These shrunken photographs were sent overseas. Once there, the tiny letters were returned to their normal size. Then they were sent to the right person.

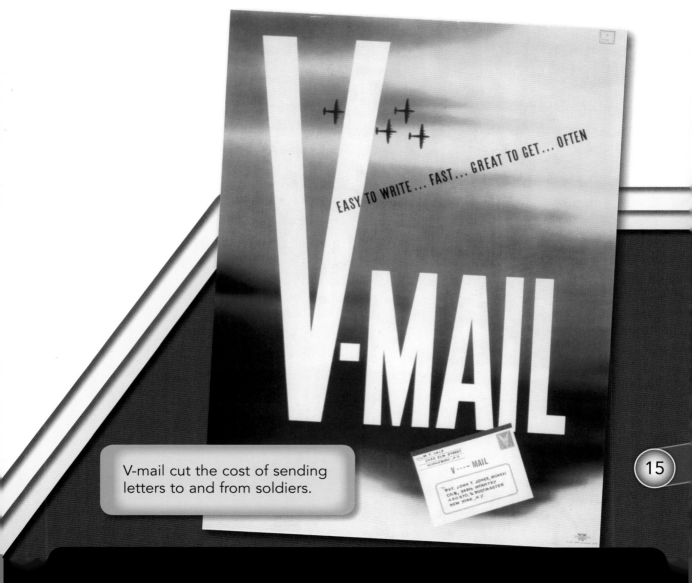

V-mail cut the cost of sending letters to and from soldiers.

Paying for the war

Fighting a war costs money. The army and navy must train men to fight. Weapons must be built.

The United States helped pay for the war with **war bonds**. A bond is an agreement to let someone borrow money. A person buying a war bond was letting the U.S. borrow money to fight the war.

The "shadow" in this poster is a "swastika." It was a symbol for Hitler's Germany.

Don't Let That Shadow Touch Them
Buy WAR BONDS

war bond agreement to let the U.S. borrow money during the war

Kids buy war stamps

Children often bought war stamps. They were just like bonds. But stamps cost less than $1.00. The stamps were pasted into stamp books. Kids would turn in the stamp books later for more than they paid for them. War stamps helped kids save money. They also helped the war effort.

The girl in this poster is putting war stamps into a stamp book.

Americans bought many types of war bonds. Some were $25 bonds. Each person paid $18.75 to get one. After ten years, the government paid them back $25. That is $6.25 more than they paid. People made money by buying war bonds.

Posters urged people to buy war bonds. Americans bought many of them. They wanted to support their troops.

Fighting the Enemy

Spies are everywhere in wartime. Many of them listen for gossip (talk about others). **Gossip** about the war can be helpful to spies.

For instance, a wife might talk about her husband's ship. She might tell a friend when it sets sail. By accident, this might put her husband in danger. The spy might overhear. He might repeat what the wife said to an enemy country. An enemy submarine could come and sink his ship.

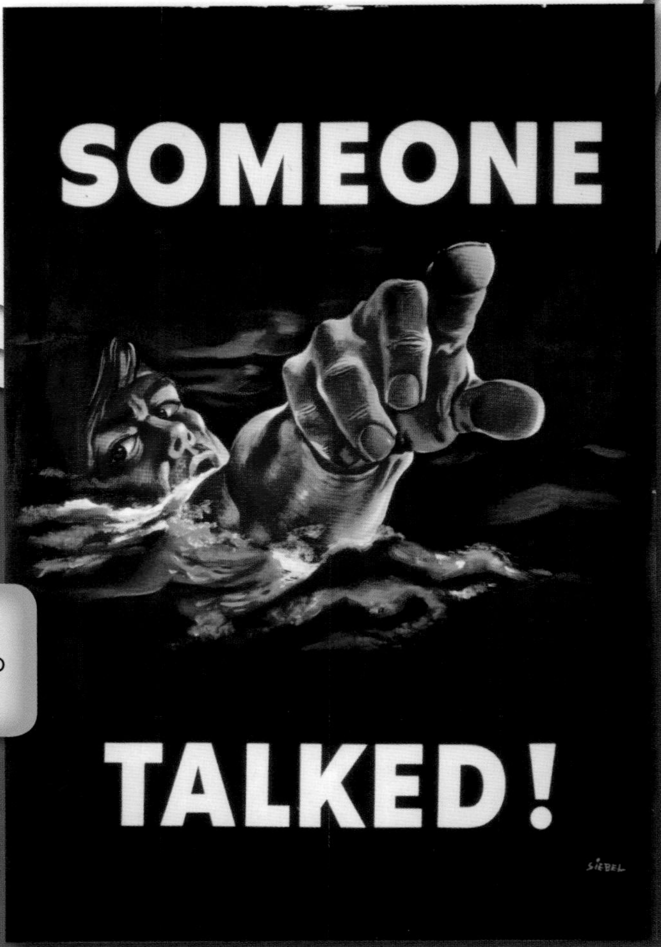

In this poster, a drowning sailor blames Americans who gossip for sinking his ship.

SOMEONE

TALKED!

SIEBEL

Careless TALK COSTS LIVES

W P A WAR SERVICES of LA.

AL DORIA

Posters like this reminded people at home not to talk about the war. Spies might be listening!

Soldiers had to watch what they wrote in letters. Their letters were **censored**. That means someone read over them. The censors might take out some details. Those details might help the enemy.

For example, a soldier might write "We fought in Rome Tuesday. But we moved on Thursday." The enemy might find that letter. They could use it to track that soldier's movements. They could kill more U.S. soldiers that way.

Posters reminded people to be quiet about details. Lives depended on it.

19

censored   reading over another person's letter in order to remove harmful details

Why we fight

Franklin Roosevelt was the U.S. president during World War II. He was the leader of the country. He knew the war would be long and hard. Some Americans lost friends and loved ones. They died in the fighting. Others were afraid of losing people.

The United States is a free country. But the **Axis** countries of Germany, Italy, and Japan were not. Roosevelt wanted to remind people why they were fighting. He came up with the Four Freedoms. The artist Norman Rockwell made these posters. People liked them a lot. They became four of the best-known posters of the war.

Freedom of Speech—People cannot be punished for saying unpopular things.

Freedom of Worship—People can choose any religious belief.

Freedom from **Want** (not having enough)—People should be able to get food, clothes, and homes.

Freedom from Fear—People do not have to worry about being attacked.

want   not having enough food, clothes, or housing

OURS...to fight for

Freedom of Speech

Freedom of Worship

Freedom from Want

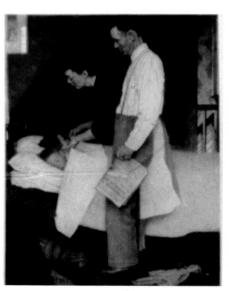

Freedom from Fear

The Four Freedoms posters were painted by Norman Rockwell. They reminded Americans why they were fighting the war.

Fighting side-by-side

The Soviet Union was one of the **Allies**. They fought on the side of Great Britain and the United States. But the Soviet Union started the war as a friend of Germany. Soviet armies even helped Hitler take over Poland.

That changed in June 1941. Hitler invaded the **Soviet Union**. The Germans attacked without warning. The Soviets were surprised. Many of their soldiers were killed. Much of their land was taken. Hitler almost won.

This Soviet poster shows the Allies beating Hitler. The other red, white, and blue flag is Great Britain's. The red flag is for the Soviet Union.

Americans (on the left) meet up with soldiers from the Soviet Union.

But Hitler forgot about the weather. Soviet winters are very cold. German soldiers did not have clothes for the cold. Their machines froze. The German army could not move.

The Soviet Union then became one of the Allies. They got weapons from Great Britain. They got them from the United States. The Soviets began to beat the Germans.

Early Soviet posters were nice to Hitler. But after the invasion, the Soviets made fun of him. The poster on page 22 shows Hitler being choked. He is being choked by the three main Allies. The flags stand for the Allies. They stand for Great Britain, the United States, and the Soviet Union.

Dropping leaflets

Most posters are meant to hang on walls. But **leaflets** were different. They often had artwork like posters. But leaflets were smaller. Also, leaflets were meant only to be read or looked at. Few people put them up on walls.

Be wise - come over to Jerry

Your pals are waiting for you in Germany, waiting for you to join them in their golf and football games.

You will live in peace and complete safety, and your relatives will rejoice to know that they will be seeing you again.

Come on over, stop fighting, make a new start!

Give yourself up to the first Jerry you see.

You will be treated well, and you will be glad to be out of it.

Have you been told the casualties up to July 15th ? Here are your own official figures :

British :	**Canadians :**	**U. S. A. :**
15.526 killed	2.089 killed	18.246 killed
46.578 wounded	9.267 wounded	54.363 wounded
9.393 missing	3.279 missing	11.877 missing
71.497	14.635	84.486

35.861

gave their lives in the first few weeks of the invasion. For the sake of the jews !

AND IT'S ONLY THE BEGINNING !

WORSE IS TO COME !

RUN THE BLOCKADE OF DEATH AND GET TO SAFETY.

AW 53

The leaflets on these pages tried to get Allied soldiers to give up. People called Germany "Jerry."

24

Both the **Allies** and the **Axis** countries used leaflets. Many were dropped from airplanes. The leaflets would float down. Then people would look them over. Leaflets had different jobs. Most were designed to make enemy soldiers give up. Often, they asked questions. They might ask, "Why should you die?" Or, they might ask, "Why not be safe and give up?"

Axis countries forbid people to read Allied leaflets. Axis leaders allowed no free speech. They were afraid of the leaflets. They feared people might side with the Allies. The punishment for keeping Allied leaflets was death. The Allies were scared of Axis leaflets, too. They were scared because they didn't want soldiers to give up.

This leaflet tried to scare Allied soldiers out of invading the beaches of Axis-controlled countries.

Winning the War

The war was a difficult time for everyone. People feared for loved ones who were fighting. They were tired of having things such as sugar, meat, and cheese **rationed**. They missed being able to buy as much as they wanted. They wanted the war to be over.

The United States used posters to keep spirits up. Some posters reminded people about why the country was at war. Others told people that things would be better after the war. But first people had to defeat the **Axis** Powers.

Posters reminded people to keep working hard until victory was won.

STAY ON THE JOB

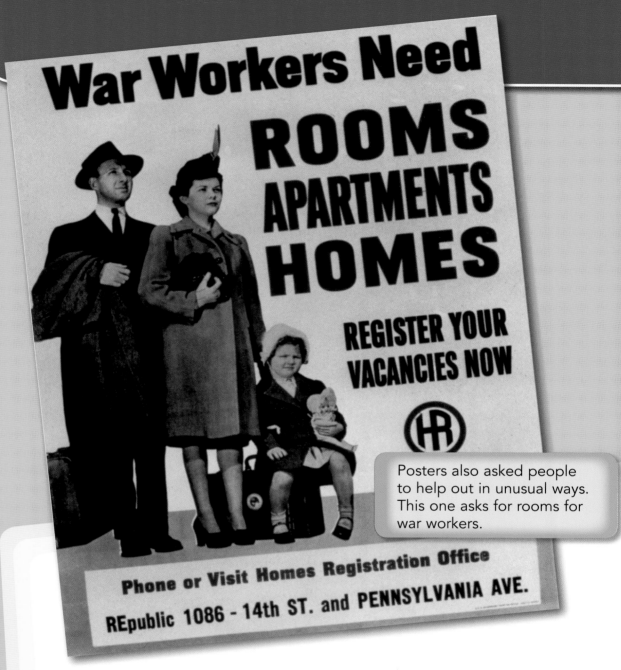

War Workers Need ROOMS APARTMENTS HOMES

REGISTER YOUR VACANCIES NOW

Posters also asked people to help out in unusual ways. This one asks for rooms for war workers.

Phone or Visit Homes Registration Office
REpublic 1086 - 14th ST. and PENNSYLVANIA AVE.

The Axis countries fought hard. But they finally gave up. Italy was the first to give up in 1944. It was followed by Germany in May 1945. Japan was the last. The Japanese surrendered in August 1945. August 14 was the last day of World War II. People all over the world were glad that the war was finally over.

Hollywood goes to war

There was no television during World War II. People went to the movies instead. Hollywood movies were very popular.

Hollywood made movies about the war. People on the **home front** liked war movies. They felt movies showed what fighting was really like. Movie makers had to be careful. They could not show too much shooting. They could not show too much blood. That would upset people.

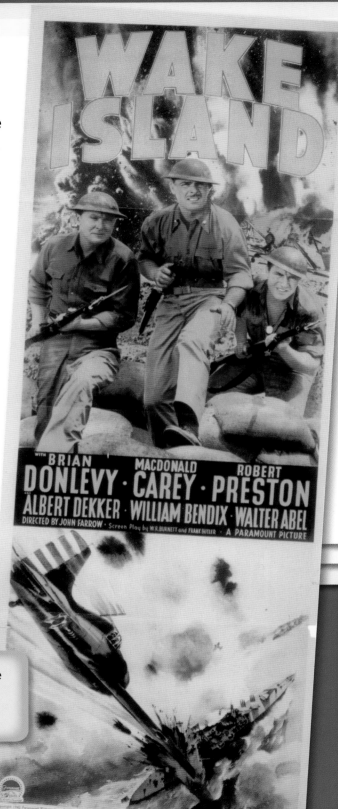

War movie posters like this made Americans look heroic.

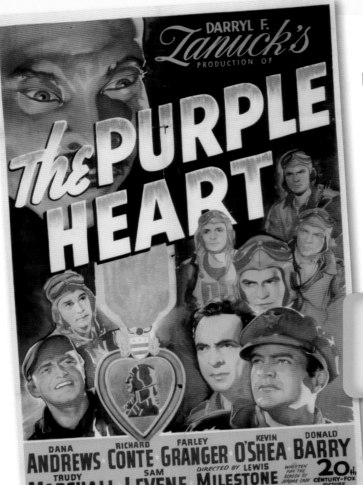

Many war movie posters had two jobs. First, they were ads. They made movies look good to watch. Second, they supported the war effort. They made the United States look strong.

A purple heart is a medal. It is given to U.S. soldiers who are wounded.

What soldiers watched

Soldiers liked movies, too. But they did not like watching war movies. They did not like to be reminded of the war. Also, they felt movies did not show what fighting was really like. Soldiers liked watching comedies and **musicals**. Comedies made them laugh. Musicals have lots of singing and dancing. They also liked to see pretty girls.

musical   movie in which there is a lot of singing and dancing

Glossary

Allies countries that sided with Great Britain during World War II. Great Britain, the Soviet Union, and the United States led the Allied forces.

Axis countries that sided with Hitler during World War II. Germany, Italy, and Japan led the Axis powers.

censored reading over another person's letter in order to remove harmful details

gossip talk about others

home front what Americans called life at home during WWII

leaflets small posters that were dropped from airplanes

musical movie in which there is a lot of singing and dancing

ration to sell something only in small amounts

Soviet Union very large country that broke into many countries in 1991. The biggest of them is Russia.

v-mail letters that were reduced and then made large again. This was done to save money.

victory garden gardens that people planted during World War II. People grew their own food.

want not having enough food, clothes, or housing

war bond agreement to let the U.S. borrow money during the war

Want to Know More?

Books to read

Adams, Simon. *Eyewitness Books: World War II*. New York: Dorling Kindersley, 2007.

Panchyk, Richard. *World War II for Kids: A History With 21 Activities*. Chicago: Chicago Review Press, 2002.

Websites

http://www.ohiohistory.org/etcetera/exhibits/kilroy/posters/index.html
Visit the Ohio Historical Society's online collection of U.S. World War II posters.

http://www.archives.gov/exhibits/powers_of_persuasion/powers_of_persuasion_home.html
This National Archives site helps explain posters. It explains why some types of posters were made and others were not.

http://www.bbc.co.uk/history/ww2children/
What was life like for kids in the war? This website helps explain what kids went through in war-torn Great Britain.

Read **Varian Fry: Hero of the Holocaust** to find out about a brave American who risked his life to rescue refugees in France.

Read **Rosie the Riveter: Women in WWII** to find out about the important role American women played during the war.

Index